Feb '24

To: Our dear
Wyatt + Ben

Inspiring Stories for Invincible Boys

A Motivational Superhero Story Book about
Overcoming Challenges, Building Confidence,
and Finding Inner Strength

Lots of Love,
Grandma & Grandpa

Hayden Fox

1

The content within this book has been derived from various sources. Please consult a licensed professional before attempting any techniques outlined in this book.

By reading this document, the reader agrees that under no circumstances is the author responsible for any losses, direct or indirect, that are incurred as a result of the use of the information contained within this document, including, but not limited to, errors, omission.

Table of Contents

A Note for Aspiring Heroes

Superpowers are amazing. Superhero stories let us imagine spectacular tales of people accomplishing the impossible with their flight, incredible strength, mind reading, supersonic speed, or any other ability we can think of. And using that same imagination is essential when solving problems, interacting with others, exploring new skills and hobbies, or just keeping your mind sharp.

It's easy to wish for powers of your own—talk about exciting! Life would be a lot easier if we had extra powers to help solve our problems. Here, though, you'll find stories of people with superpowers learning to be brave, thoughtful, resilient, clever, and compassionate. Remember that through all the excitement, close calls, and chaos, it's not fantastic powers that make a hero—it's how you behave.

The Hidden Grove Academy

Mr. Hart: The headmaster of the Hidden Grove Academy. Has a reputation for being old and wise. Since he looks younger than he is, no one is quite sure exactly how old (or how wise), but he's always thoughtful and fair.

The Empty Hand: A group of students at the Hidden Grove Academy who have innate, supernatural abilities they must learn to control if they want to be heroes.

- **Grace:** A tall, popular boy with white, feathered wings and the ability to heal anyone he touches. Takes his role mending other students seriously and keeps everyone safe.

- **Fade:** A boy with the ability to teleport and whose afterimages are quite dazzling. He goes to class when he really must, but he'd rather be playing sports or practicing martial arts.

- **Aura:** A psychic who hears everyone's thoughts, whether she wants to or not. It's hard for her to focus, but she's clever and cunning when she does.

- **Echo**: A driven, athletic boy who can project his voice and create shockwaves and vibrations with his words. Gets himself into trouble by rushing into things, but he's used to thinking fast to find a way out.

- **Titan**: A giant of a boy, covered in muscles and far larger than anyone else at the Hidden Grove Academy. He flies and he's invincible, so he gets asked to do the jobs no one else can. He doesn't like fighting, though, and would rather use his strength to help.

The Steel Heart: a group of students at the Hidden Grove Academy who are adept at harnessing science and technology, or who've gained abilities because of science gone wrong (or right!).

- **Scale**: He has amazing speed and agility, but he's still getting used to his powers. He's worried about fitting in with his classmates now that he's covered in green skin with claws on his hands and feet, a forked tongue, and a long reptilian tail.

- **Splendor**: A tough stocky boy with long unkempt hair who can channel electricity. He uses a special suit to create energy blasts.

- **Tink**: Mad scientist in training. The youngest student at the Hidden Grove Academy who's always working on something for his classmates.

- **Jack**: Good at everything he touches. Not the best, but much better than average. Sometimes sad that other students have flashier, more noticeable powers, even though he tries not to let it bother him. Always helping Tink with new inventions.

- **Mach**: Machines talk to him, help him out, and follow his instructions. Together, they're ready for anything.

Scale and the Hanging Keys

Scale was not the most popular student at the Hidden Grove Academy. Something had gone wrong when he was a baby—his parents would never quite say what it was—and he had changed from a regular boy into a sort of boy-lizard. He was covered in green skin, and he had a forked tongue, pointed teeth, a long reptilian tail, and claws instead of fingernails. He didn't remember what it was like not to be a boy-lizard, as he had been so young when the change had happened.

His parents had named him Anthony when he was born, but everyone at the Hidden Grove Academy took on nicknames that matched their powers. After other students saw how good he was at climbing, they exclaimed, "Look how fast he scaled that wall!" and nicknamed him Scale. Of course, he was also covered in green scales, so both his classmates and his teachers seemed to appreciate the pun.

Everyone at the Academy was strange, fantastic, and unique in their own way, so they'd accepted him like they would accept any other student. But Scale still felt self-conscious about how he looked, and today was his opportunity to prove himself.

It was the end of the school year, which meant it was time for the yearly competition. The competition was all in good fun and was intended to allow students to let their abilities loose while providing special challenges, but the students took it very seriously. There were two teams who participated in five different contests: The Empty Hand versus The Steel Heart. Scale was on The Steel Heart, and he was up first for the racing contest.

He looked over at the student he would be racing against, a tall boy named Grace who had giant, feathery wings. Had he gotten his nickname because he looked so graceful as he easily flew around the school grounds? Or because he had a habit of (literally!) swooping in to save people when they were in trouble? Scale didn't know—Grace was older than he was and already had his nickname when Scale arrived at the Academy.

If that wasn't enough, Grace was extremely popular. On top of being quite handsome with his beautiful wings, his touch could make other students heal rapidly. It was an incredibly useful skill to have, since every student could breathe fire, or fly, or shoot freezing lasers from their eyes, or perform some other ability that was equal parts awesome and dangerous. There were a lot of accidental bumps and bruises and injuries that needed healing.

Scale and Grace's task today was to race up a giant tree and retrieve the treasure at the top. Scale's team had chosen him because he was by far the best climber of any of them, but he didn't have wings like Grace. Still, he was going to do everything he could to win.

Their principal, Mr. Hart was acting as the referee. He looked like a young man with his short brown hair, dark t-shirt that showed off his muscles, and a thin pair of wire glasses. But the rumor was that he was much, much older than he looked. Scale figured that wasn't surprising in a school where everyone had some ability or another that made them more than human.

"Your instructions are simple," Mr. Hart said. "Climb the tree, overcome any obstacles you find, and be the first one to collect the treasure. Are you ready?"

Both boys nodded. The tree was huge and had so many branches and leaves that Scale couldn't see the top. He was nervous.

"Begin!" Mr. Hart yelled.

Grace launched himself into the air and flew toward the top of the tree. It was hopeless, Scale thought. But he wasn't going to give up, so he sprinted toward the tree, took a flying leap, and pulled himself up onto the first branch. He jumped to the next branch, and then the next, then scrambled up the trunk to another branch. Chips of wood flew through the air around him. Suddenly Scale saw the glint of metal and something hanging from a branch: a pair of metal keys. One of them had the symbol for his team—a steampunk mechanical heart for The Steel Heart. The other key had a glowing open palm to represent the opposing team, The Empty Hand. Scale took his key and left the other one alone. Maybe he had a chance after all.

Scale tried holding the key in one hand, but it made it hard to grab the branches he needed. Then he tried holding the key with his tail, but his tail was another useful limb to climb with so that still slowed him down. Scale spotted a vine snaking over a branch and tore it loose. He tied the vine around the key, considered wearing it like a necklace, and finally decided to lash it tightly to his arm instead. Much better.

He encountered a variety of traps as he kept climbing, but they were mostly intended to be a distraction. A flock of magical birds flew out at him, then exploded into colorful fireworks. A branch turned into a snake when he grabbed it, but slithered away harmlessly when Scale let go. Large, shimmering, buttercup-yellow flowers dumped a sticky rainbow liquid all over him that disappeared within a few minutes. If he wasn't racing, the tree would actually be a fun place to explore, but Scale stayed focused.

Above him, he could see another pair of sparkling keys. He moved toward them quickly. Then he saw, further up the tree, something large... and it was coming at him fast, half-climbing, and half-falling down the tree. A pair of wings unfurled to slow the fall. It was Grace.

"He must have found the locked treasure, and now he's looking for the keys," Scale mumbled to himself. He wondered briefly how many keys there were. If Grace had flown to the top of the tree, he might already know.

Scale lunged toward the keys above him. His claws had just brushed against them when Grace crashed into him, falling fast. The boys tumbled through the branches. They grappled for a moment until Scale stuck out a hand, sunk his claws into the tree, and came to a sliding stop, leaving four long gashes behind. Grace hung on to Scale, hitting the trunk with a grunt and shaking his head. They both started climbing again with the second key just in sight above them.

Scale was faster—but just barely. He grabbed his key at the same time that Grace grabbed his ankle. Scale gave a shake, but Grace held on.

"Let go!" Scale yelled.

Grace grunted and held on. Scale was desperate. He knew that once he got this key, Grace would only have the key at the bottom of the tree to retrieve. Then he could fly to the top again and win while Scale was still climbing. However, Scale had an idea that would buy him some time. He grabbed the other key, gave a mischievous smile to Grace, and then threw the key as far as he could.

"That's not fair!" Grace cried. But he let go of Scale and flew off to try and catch the key before it was out of sight and nearly impossible to find.

Scale ignored him and lashed the second key to his arm next to the first. As he kept climbing, he came across a thin slime on the branches that made it impossible to move quickly. Whenever he tried to rush, he started slipping.

He stretched to grab a branch that was a bit too far and his fingers slipped right over it, almost causing him to fall out of the tree completely. Scale knew he needed to hurry, but not so fast that he lost his grip and fell. He took a deep breath and moved deliberately from one branch to the next, focusing on each small movement.

Finally, he saw a third key. This key hung by itself, so Grace must have already grabbed his. The problem was, the key hung around the stem of a giant, snapping, hungry-looking Venus flytrap. This was no ordinary plant. It had no eyes, of course, but the flowerhead twisted one way and the other quickly, as though looking for something to eat. There was no time to hesitate. Scale swung in and attempted to grab his prize, but the plant snapped at him and he had to jump away again. On the second try he managed to get his hand around the key, but the plant clamped down on him.

"Ouch!" Scale yelped, giving the plant a hard shake. It let go and hissed at him as he scrambled away.

He could see the top of the tree now, although he still had a bit of a climb left. He could feel numbness in his arm where the flytrap had bitten him, and before long he couldn't rely on that hand to climb. But he was close. He was there. He was going to win.

He saw a door at the top of the tree, festooned with three keyholes and the Steel Heart's insignia. Relief washed over him—until he heard a shout of triumph. Grace was above him, wings outstretched, holding a large red ruby he hadn't had before. Scale climbed the last few feet and put his keys into the keyholes carefully, but when he opened the door, he saw the nook was already empty. On the other side, a door with The Empty Hand's insignia hung open.

Grace had flown away from him, caught the second key, found the first key near the bottom, and flown up to the top of the tree before him, just like Scale had feared. He had given the race his all, and he had still lost.

"Good race," Scale muttered, feeling dejected, jealous, and a little angry.

"You too," Grace said. "Really. I thought it would be easy for me, no offense. But I had all the advantages and you nearly won anyway."

"My arm hurts," Scale said. How did you get past the fly trap so easily?

"I didn't," Grace admitted. "I tried to fly in, but I wasn't fast enough. It bit my wing, and I thought I was going to crash for a minute. But I can heal myself, too."

Scale couldn't help but wonder if he would have won if he had healing abilities like Grace and could have used both arms for the final climb. It didn't seem fair.

"I didn't stand a chance," he grumbled.

"Are you kidding? You were amazing," Grace declared. "You didn't win this time, but with your determination, you're going to have a lot of victories in your life. I know it. Here, let me heal your arm."

Scale extended his hand and Grace gave him a firm handshake. While their hands were clasped, Scale could feel a tingle in his arm as it started to heal. By the time they let go, he felt as good as new.

"Seriously, I'm proud of you," Grace said. "Proud of both of us. I wonder what the other competitions will look like."

Grace offered to carry Scale out of the tree, and Scale accepted. They floated down to their waiting teammates. Grace's team met him with wild cheers and clapped him on the back, while Scale's team met him with subdued condolences. They were kind to him, but they'd really wanted to win, too.

Behind him, though, he could hear Grace telling the story of his victory... and it made Scale sound amazing. Grace admitted to his teammates that he'd messed up by trying to fly first instead of climb, and that Scale was stronger than him when they'd crashed into each other. Grace even told them he was impressed that Scale had thought of throwing his key away, and said he was lucky to have reached it before it fell into a nearby pond and made them lose the contest. Scale could see the other students looking at him in admiration as they listened to Grace's tale.

Scale had tried his best, and he'd lost anyway. He felt like he deserved to win since he had given it everything he had. But, he realized, Grace had given it his all as well, and there could only be one winner. Scale did his best to remember that his effort was what he should be proud of, not a victory or a loss. Scale reminded himself that he may have lost today, but there would be many chances of victories in the future, so long as he remained determined and resilient.

Fade and the Final Blink

Fade walked down a corridor toward the outdoor yard the students had nicknamed The Arena. His team, The Empty Hand, was already up by one point. To win the next point, he'd have to beat his opponent in a sparring match. He didn't know who he would be fighting yet, but long before he'd discovered his abilities, his parents had signed him up for many different sports—football, track and field, and boxing were among his favorites. He liked competition, and he felt comfortable with the pressure to win. A few years ago, when he was feeling nervous about joining the Academy, his father had told him a saying that would forever stick with him: You can't make diamonds without pressure.

Fade blinked down the hallway, disappearing and then reappearing several feet ahead in an instant. Every time he blinked, it left an image of him behind, like what you'd see if you looked at something too bright for too long. Then, the image would fade out of existence.

When he got close to the end of the hall, he took a deep, calming breath.

Then, he stepped out into the courtyard.

The Arena was dusty. The dirt floor was perfect for sparring, and the space was surrounded by a red brick wall. There was no point in decorating it, since it was routinely set on fire, frozen, blasted with storms, or subjected to a dozen other disasters as students practiced their abilities. Today, everyone would be watching Fade and his sparring partner.

Fade's opponent entered from the other side of The Arena. His name was Splendor; he was a stocky boy with long, unkempt hair. He had a jumpsuit on, similar to his, except it was covered with thick wires that looked like metallic veins. Fade had seen Splendor fight before, and he was good at it. He had the ability to channel energy, and he could project it by using the wires to fire bright beams from his hands. If Fade couldn't find a way to get past those beams, he wouldn't stand a chance.

Mr. Hart called down to them, his voice magically amplified. "Splendor and Fade, you will be fighting today. You win when your opponent can't fight back anymore, or when they give up. Are you ready?"

They all knew the rules well. Students did this regularly as a way to play with and test each other. Their classmate Grace was in high demand here, ready to rush out and heal everyone after they roughed each other up.

"Good luck to you both," Mr. Hart called.

Splendor raised his arms immediately and shot a red beam toward Fade. It was more of a test shot than anything else, and it was easy for Fade to jump away from. Fade ran toward Splendor as fast as he could, closing the distance quickly and blinking to the side to help him avoid the lasers. They hit the dirt or the brick wall with a sizzle and left little wisps of smoke behind, but Fade stayed focused on Splendor. He couldn't teleport all the way to him in a single blink, but if he could get close enough, he'd have a shot at winning.

He was almost there when he had to teleport away from an energy blast. Splendor was quick to react, shooting another blast right where Fade had teleported. Fade flew backwards and landed in the dirt. Looking up at the sky, he struggled to get his bearings and then blinked away as another energy beam landed where he had just been. Fade was sore and covered in dirt. He'd been able to take one energy blast, but one more of those could mean the end of the competition.

"Okay then," Fade said to himself.

He ran toward Splendor again, this time being less predictable. He would blink forward so the blasts sailed harmlessly behind him, or at strange angles so follow-up shots were wild guesses. Students cheered as The Arena became a blur of flashing energy beams and transparent copies of Fade in his colorful outfit.

Finally, Fade was close enough to blink behind Splendor, who couldn't turn quickly because of his bulky uniform. Fade shoved him onto the ground and then jumped on top of him, hoping to pin the other boy down. He wasn't as large as Splendor, but he had a lot more practice grappling.

Splendor rolled onto his back, and Fade realized he was smiling. Fade smiled too. Sure, they were fighting, but they were also having fun. Whatever the end result was, Fade was sure they would be laughing together soon—and probably asking for a rematch.

"Bye!" Splendor said to Fade. Energy beams shot from the bottom of Splendor's boots, this time orange-white with heat. The force of the blast shot Splendor away along the ground, spraying dirt in every direction. It wasn't pretty, but it separated them again and gave Splendor his advantage back.

There was a moment of quiet as dust settled and smoke cleared, and then the boys ran at each other again. Splendor let out a loud, war-like yell and his teammates cheered in support. But their cheering stopped when Fade suddenly blinked behind Splendor and pushed him to the ground again. Splendor tried to shoot at Fade from the ground, but Fade blinked around the beams.

He jumped back on top of Splendor, and the two rolled around in the dirt. Splendor was bigger and heavier, but every time he was pinned, Fade would blink behind him again to put himself back on top. Finally Fade grabbed one of Splendor's arms, wondering if he could dismantle the weapons.

Suddenly, there was a massive burst of light. Fade blinked away reflexively to avoid the blast, but he landed hard. He couldn't see well for a second, having been momentarily blinded by the bright flash. He could hear the students cheering again. He blinked around The Arena several times in quick succession—not paying attention to where he was going, but just trying to keep moving to avoid being hit. He could see there was a small crater where he had just been, smoke rising out of it. He realized there was smoke rising off him as well. He avoided any direct hits, but the near-misses and explosions were enough to knock him off his feet several times.

"Is that enough?" Splendor called out to him.

"Never!" Fade yelled back. Years of practice meant it would take more than a few bumps and bruises for him to surrender, especially since he knew he could be healed as good as new once the fight was over.

Next, Splendor used his boots to emit a continuous energy beam and lift himself high into the air. It must have taken a lot of power, but it meant he was now significantly out of reach.

"That's going to be a problem," Fade said. He could taste the dust in the air and wished he hadn't opened his mouth.

Splendor began raining energy blasts down onto the field. Fade blinked from one spot to another and managed to avoid them. He couldn't keep this up forever though, so he decided to try something he had always been too nervous to do before: He blinked up. Fade found himself ten feet in the air and falling rapidly. *Wow, it actually worked!* he thought and landed awkwardly.

If I can do it once, I can do it as many times as I want, he thought.

I know I'm capable and I believe in myself.

I can do this!

He blinked upward, ready to be in the air this time. Before he could hit the ground, he blinked a second time, then again and again. As long as he was quick and focused, Fade realized he could teleport in succession and rise into the air.

Soon, Fade was close enough to Splendor to blink over to him and he grabbed on, arms around the bigger boy's neck with his legs wrapped around his waist. The weight was too much, and Splendor couldn't keep the boots pointed at the ground as he tumbled over. They sailed through the air erratically, half fighting each other and half simply trying to stabilize.

Fade grabbed one of the main wires on the suit and yanked hard. There was a spark and a sputter, and the beams of energy stopped firing. Fade could still feel Splendor's energy crackling around him, but without the suit, there was no way to focus it.

They tumbled toward the ground below, but at the last moment, Fade blinked away. Splendor crashed with a heavy thud and another spray of dirt and dust.

When Fade got closer, he saw that Splendor was laughing. He was grimacing in pain, but he seemed to be okay.

"Okay, okay, that's enough," Splendor admitted. "You win this one."

Fade offered him a hand to help him up, and Splendor leaned on him heavily as Grace flew down from the crowd to greet them. He helped Splendor first, who breathed a sigh of relief as his injuries and soreness washed away. Grace healed Fade next. Although he didn't need as much help as Splendor, it was still welcome. Both fighters were covered in dirt and dust, but they felt as strong and healthy as when they had started.

"That. Was. So. Cool," Splendor said. "I didn't know you could fly!"

"Me either," Fade said. "I never tried it before today, but I had to figure out how to get up to you! Where did you get that awesome suit?"

"Tink built it for me," Splendor said. "He's always building something or another, and energy blasts are a lot more useful than the sparks and fireworks I can make without it. But I think he's going to have to make another one after what you did to this one."

Mr. Hart approached them and waited patiently for them to finish speaking. "Both of you are impressive fighters," he said. "But I'm more impressed by your sportsmanship and camaraderie. Even when things were at their most intense, you treated each other with respect. Everyone would do well to remember that lesson. Regardless of the winner, you've both conducted yourself like heroes."

Fade felt proud. He had believed in himself and didn't give up, no matter how hard things got or how many times he got knocked down. Because of it, his team had now built up a two-point lead. He didn't rub it in, though, because he didn't want his friend to feel bad. He knew the most important thing was that they'd had fun and gotten some practice to help them learn to use their powers better. Fade had a strong feeling that as long as he remained determined and focused, and never stopped believing in himself, he could become one of the greatest heroes the Academy had ever seen.

Tink and the Psychic Song

Tink was the youngest student at the Hidden Grove Academy. He'd started school two years earlier than anyone else, mostly because his parents didn't know what else to do with him. By the time he was seven, he was building all manner of contraptions and inventions, from tiny robots to deliver him toast in the mornings to huge floating platforms he used as a treehouse (since their yard didn't have any trees). When neighbors started to complain, his parents knew Tink needed to be somewhere where he would have the freedom to learn and build as much as he liked. Since he was always tinkering with something, his classmates quickly gave him the nickname Tink. He leaned into it, designing a pair of steampunk goggles in place of his previous glasses and a blue lab coat to put over his clothes. The new look made him happy.

He was nervous about the contest today. Usually, Tink just worked on whatever project caught his fancy, and when he was no longer interested, he would abandon it for something else. His room—as well as some classrooms and teachers' offices—were cluttered with half-finished projects, blueprints, and spare parts, each waiting to be noticed again so they could be turned into inventions like nothing the world had never seen. But today, Tink would have to stay focused on a single task.

He would be competing against another student to solve a puzzle. They would be locked in a room together, and they each had to think their way out. Whoever solved the last puzzle first would get the single key that would let them out and score their team a point. Tink's team was already down by two points, so he really needed to win this round to keep them in it.

Tink got into the elevator—which he had actually built after getting tired of rushing up and down stairs all day—and waited. A few moments later, his opponent Aura came in and stood next to him. She was a fair bit older than Tink was, and it intimidated him. She wore her Empty Hand uniform, except it was different than the rest of her teammates, much like how Tink's was. Rather than a jumpsuit, she wore pants and a full sleeves shirt. His favorite part about her outfit though was her long hooded cloak, which felt unique much like his own lab coat did.

"Don't worry, kid, you're going to do fine," Aura said. "But I'm not going to let you win."

Tink felt a flush of nervousness, but he would have to get used to it, because Aura was a psychic. Anything he thought, she could hear as clearly as if he'd said it out loud.

"We'll see about that," Tink said. Although, he was not reassured.

The elevator took them down to the basement of the building. They walked together to the end of the hall. Tink wanted to make some small talk with Aura, but he didn't know how. He realized she could hear his thoughts and she knew that he wanted to talk but was too nervous, and that only made him even more nervous than before. Aura smiled softly. She must be used to that kind of reaction.

They entered the room meant for them, which was a mess. There was clutter everywhere. Tink felt more comfortable once he saw the room, since it reminded him of his many workshops. There was an order to the chaos, though, as there were areas of the room that had clearly been set up to be explored.

"I'm used to hearing a dozen thoughts at once, but I'm not going to be able to make sense of this mess," Aura said. "I should have been signed up for one of the other competitions instead."

Don't worry, you're going to do fine, Tink thought. *But I'm not going to let you win.* He winked at her.

Aura laughed. "See? Now you're getting it. Smart kid."

Mr. Hart appeared before them, except it wasn't actually Mr. Hart—it was a translucent projection of him. Tink noticed that Mr. Hart seemed to have a wide array of powers that he used casually. Even though the kids at Hidden Grove all had unusual abilities, they generally had one special ability, or maybe two if they were lucky. Tink thought that Mr. Hart could do anything he wanted to, and he felt very lucky that Mr. Hart had decided to be one of his teachers.

"You need to escape from this room," Mr. Hart's apparition said. "No fighting with each other, and you can't use your powers or any inventions to get through the door. Solving each puzzle will give you one part of the key.

Any questions?"

Simple rules for a complicated game, Tink thought.

"No kidding," Aura said. "I'm not even good at stuff like this."

The door closed behind them, Mr. Hart's image disappeared, and they began.

Tink hurried over to one of the puzzles, and Aura chose another. A grid of letters were carved into a large, wooden desk. Tink scanned the letters but couldn't find any words, even if he looked vertically or backwards. That would be too easy, he supposed.

He looked around on the desk and everything seemed pretty normal. A computer, a pen and paper, some letters... even an old-timey typewriter off to one side. Wasn't it a bit strange, having so many ways to write all on one desk? Tink took a closer look and noticed a few of the keys were missing from the typewriter. The O, X, and G keys had been popped off.

Aura called out from behind him. "Ugh! I hate puzzles like this. People think because I'm good with one thing with my brain, I must be smart at everything. It doesn't work like that."

Tink didn't know what to say, so he ignored her and kept working. He felt like he should say something, but he loved puzzles and he really wanted to win.

The computer keyboard had the same issue—a few of the keys had popped off. Tink grabbed the paper and the pen, went back to the letter grid, and tried writing out only the missing letters. It was gibberish. He almost gave up on the idea when he noticed something. On one of the lines, if he wrote out the letters that *weren't* missing, it spelled out "SEVEN." But the other lines still didn't make any sense. He must be missing a clue.

He looked at the letter on the desk and discovered a lovely poem about a summer day at the beach. But when he looked closer, some letters were missing here, too. The word "waves" appeared several times, but the "a" was always missing, and there were a few other letters that had been consistently left out of other words too. He read the poem again and wrote down the missing letters, thankful he'd always been good at spelling.

SEVEN, FIVE, THREE, NINE, the puzzle now revealed. Tink looked around once more but couldn't see anywhere he could enter a code or use the numbers. He checked under the chair and the keyboard, turned the typewriter over as its internal pieces clattered in protest, and then opened the desk drawer. It was there waiting for him... a small wooden box secured by a simple combination lock.

He laughed at himself for missing the obvious, but felt proud of his problem-solving success. The lock popped open as soon as he put in the code he'd discovered. A glowing, green wisp of smoke rose from the box, snaked its way over to the door, and disappeared. Then, the box snapped shut and locked again.

Tink walked over to the other puzzle, the one Aura wasn't working on. There were musical instruments suspended in the air, held ready to play as if by an unseen orchestra. But before he could figure out what he should do, he noticed that Aura had left her puzzle and gone over to the one he'd just finished. She didn't look at the puzzle at all. She opened the drawer, entered the combination, and a purple wisp of smoke rose from the box and traveled to the door.

Tink froze. *She can read my mind*, he thought.

Yep, Aura thought. *You use your talents, and I'll use mine. Sorry.*

Tink realized he had "heard" Aura in his mind, but she hadn't actually said anything out loud. *You can send your thoughts to other people, too?* he thought questioningly.

When I want to, Aura thought back to Tink.

It was a strange feeling, like his ears and brain couldn't quite make sense of it, and it made it harder for him to focus on other things. If that was how it felt to Aura when she heard everyone else's thoughts, it must be really hard for her to be around other people. He assumed she heard his thoughts about her, too, but she didn't say anything back to him.

Tink set that aside to ask about later and hurried over to the puzzle Aura had already worked on. It was a blinking color pattern in front of a mirror. There was a panel with a variety of colors on it as well, which lit up when they were touched. Tink tried a few different combinations and tried copying the flashing pattern, but nothing happened.

On the floor, he noticed a large circle that had all the same colors as the panel. Arrows pointed across it, so it was easy to identify which colors were opposite each other on the color wheel.

Oh, that's easy. Tink thought. *It wants the colors opposite from the pattern, like a mirror image.* It took a minute for him to get the hang of pushing the right panels, but once he did, he was able to enter the correct pattern. The mirror released a wisp of green smoke that went to the door, just like the first.

"Don't be so smug," Aura said. "I couldn't figure it out. Not everyone is as smart as you."

"I wasn't being smug!" Tink protested. "Stop reading my thoughts if you don't want to know them."

"Trust me, I wish I could," Aura said. "It doesn't exactly turn off."

She seemed annoyed that she hadn't figured out the puzzle herself, but she went over, practiced a few times to get the colors right, and then claimed her prize.

Tink went back over to the music puzzle and closed his eyes. He needed a plan, or Aura would be able to hear his thoughts while he figured out the puzzle. If she did that and then solved the last piece before him, there would be nothing he could do.

Was there a way to keep his thoughts to himself? he wondered.

"No," Aura said. "Sorry again. Are you any good with music? My parents wanted me to play piano, but when I practiced, all I could hear was them thinking about how bad I was, so I gave up."

Tink resisted the temptation to look at the puzzle. He didn't want to accidentally give Aura a clue. "My parents were a lot more supportive. I think you're cool and I want to hang out and talk some more, but first I have to win this for my team."

"I appreciate that you said that out loud," Aura said. "I like the honesty."

"Me too," Tink said. "Although, you'd hear it anyway."

That's when it occurred to him. *Whatever I think, she'll hear anyway.* He opened his eyes. He looked at the puzzle, careful not to focus on anything too long. In his mind, he thought: *Ducks. Big ducks, little ducks, ducks with cowboy hats. Mighty ducks, meek ducks, friendly ducks, vampire ducks with pointy teeth.* As he kept his thoughts about ducks at the front of his mind, he looked at each musical instrument. He wasn't trying to solve anything; he was just gathering information.

"Stop that," Aura said. "Ducks are cute, but how many can you really need, anyway?"

Tink started thinking about singing to the ducks. *How much is that ducky in the window, the one with the fluffily tail?*

"Fluffily isn't even a word!" Aura said, giving her head a vigorous shake.

Tink sang a song to himself about ducks and grapes, amusing himself by mixing up the lines and adding rhymes that didn't really work. Aura sighed and pinched the bridge of her nose. It seemed to be working. He was making it harder for her to concentrate.

Tink noticed sheet music nearby with the name of their school song at the top. Aura was so distracted by the ducks that she didn't even "hear" what he'd discovered. Tink grabbed the stick that conductors use (he knew it had a name, but he couldn't remember what it was and didn't want to think about it too hard while Aura was listening in) and pointed to each instrument in the correct order to make the song come to life. When the final instrument, a large cello, played its tune, it released a final wisp of green smoke. When the smoke reached the door, the door opened on its own. He had won!

"You're really smart. That was amazing thinking," Aura said.

"Thank you," Tink said. He blushed.

"I'd still like to hang out some time," Aura said. "But if I catch you trying to make me think about ducks again, I'm out."

Tink laughed. They walked out together, and he felt a rush of relief because he had been so worried about losing. He knew it was important to believe in yourself, but it was so much harder when you were trying something difficult. He knew that it was always important to remember his strengths— being thoughtful, clever, and creative—and they would always be able to carry him to victory, regardless of the circumstances. However, it was much easier to believe that after he'd already won. He resolved that in the future, he would always remember to trust in his abilities, even in the most difficult moments.

Aura heard all his thoughts. "You really were," she said. "Thoughtful, clever, and creative, I mean. Keep working on that, and I bet you can achieve anything."

Jack and the Daring Rescue

Jack always felt like an outsider at school. It had taken him a long time to realize he had special powers. Even after he found out, he was disappointed his powers weren't big and splashy like the other students' powers, such as the ability to shapeshift or shoot lightning or breathe fire. He didn't have anything like that. On top of it all, he was the only student at the Hidden Grove Academy without a nickname.

Jack was great at everything. Not perfect, but good enough to impress other students whenever they did things together. Any time he tried something new, he could just tell how it worked. Whether it was fixing a computer or shooting a basketball or painting a picture, he excelled at whatever he tried. His teachers back at his regular school had often remarked that he was a natural at whatever the current task was. However, they then usually scolded him when he would move on to something else, rather than focus on any one particular talent.

Jack was the name he had been born with, and when the other students at the Academy saw him easily learning everything from juggling to writing poetry, they remarked that he was a "Jack of all trades." So, they left him with the name Jack. He wanted a name that felt powerful and evocative, like the other kids all had. Instead, he was just Jack. And now, with his team losing two to one with only two contests left, he needed to win if they wanted a chance in the final round.

It wouldn't be easy. The other boy in the competition, Echo, had always impressed Jack. He was a wiry, athletic boy with short dark hair. Echo held himself with confidence; whenever there was a chance for the students to use their powers, Echo was more likely than not to find himself on the winning team. His ability seemed simple—he could create far-reaching sounds with his voice. But, whenever Jack saw him at school, Echo could be seen using his ability in new and creative ways. He would use a loud yell to knock over a tree, or push himself off the ground with a glider and the force of his voice. It always surprised other students, but Echo had been using his unique voice for so long that it seemed to be as natural to him as walking.

They met far from the school grounds. It seemed like an odd place to meet, but as Jack walked out into the field, he saw that an entire castle had sprung up seemingly out of nowhere. There was a moat, a drawbridge, thick stone walls, towers with spires and waving flags—everything.

"Wow, I've never seen a real castle before," Jack remarked.

Echo was busy stretching his muscles, jogging in place, and warming up his voice. "You still haven't," he said. "Mr. Hart probably used magic to put this here, and it'll be gone again tomorrow."

Echo's reply felt dismissive, so Jack didn't respond. Whether the castle had been built by hand or by magic, he still thought it was cool. Other students had gathered to watch, and even though most of the other students seemed just as impressed by the castle as Jack was, Echo's comment still hurt his feelings.

The castle drawbridge lowered, and Mr. Hart came out. The bridge rose on its own again once Mr. Hart had crossed. He walked through the field casually, seeming to enjoy the light breeze and fair weather. The students waited anxiously as he approached.

"Hurry up!" Echo called, his voice carrying over the wind. "We want to start."

Mr. Hart did not hurry. If anything, Jack thought, he slowed down after Echo's demand. Jack tried to stay calm while he waited, and eventually Mr. Hart reached them.

"I've finished the preparations for this event," he said. "In a few moments, Jack and Echo will breach the castle, rescue the prisoners, and bring them back here. Whoever returns first—with their prisoner safe and sound—is the winner."

"Got it," Echo said. "Smash in, find the prisoners, get out. Piece of cake."

Mr. Hart looked pointedly at Echo. "Confidence is important. *If* you have the skill to earn it, and the wisdom to use it well." Echo didn't seem to notice that he was being chastised. Mr. Hart continued, "Good luck to you both. You may begin."

The suddenness caught Jack by surprise. Echo was already sprinting toward the castle. Jack rushed after him, but not at full speed. He had a feeling he would need his energy, and Echo was faster than him anyway. He wasn't going to win in a foot race. When he reached the castle, Echo was already there, yelling at the drawbridge. There was a powerful boom with each yell, but the bridge held steady.

Jack looked around. There was no way to open the entrance from this side of the moat, and the moat was too wide for him to jump across. Could he swim? The moat appeared to be as much sludge and mud as actual water, so probably not.

"You know what?" Echo said. "Who needs a door when you have a window? See you on the other side."

Echo unfurled a small glider, lowered his head, and with a long, low hum, rose into the air. As Echo flew toward the castle, Jack heard someone yell, "They attack us from the air!" From the top of the castle, soldiers threw large nets weighed down by heavy stones toward them. Jack was able to easily step aside and avoid the net headed toward him, but another net caught Echo by surprise, and he tumbled down into the moat with a wet, dirty splash.

That would slow him down, but Jack knew it wouldn't keep Echo busy for long. There had to be a way to cross. The only thing nearby, besides the grass and the moat, was the rope net. Jack removed the weights and tore at the net, tying the individual ropes together until he had one long, thick rope. Nearby, he could still hear Echo yelling and splashing as he pulled himself out of the muck.

Jack formed a loop at one end of the rope and threw it across, aiming at part of the castle where a stone was protruding from the wall. The makeshift lasso found its target and held tight. Other students accused him of being "lucky," but they never seemed to have the same accusations when using their own powers. Jack pushed the negative thoughts out of his mind, got a running start, and leapt toward the castle.

He sailed through the air and slammed into the hard castle wall. It shocked him, and he almost let go of the rope. Jack looked down and saw Echo attempting to climb up the side of the moat, through the mud. He definitely did not look happy. Jack, however, continued to scale the wall, pulled himself onto a ledge, and climbed through a narrow window.

"Thanks for the tip," Jack said to himself.

The inside of the castle was dark. Jack had expected guards but there were none around—at least not in this room. Tapestries hung on the walls, but there wasn't enough light to examine them in detail. Stone stairs looked like they led both up to the towers and down to... the kitchens? The dungeons?

The stables? He wished he knew which way to go.

Jack moved through several rooms. There was an audience chamber with a throne, where he picked up a heavy stone scepter. He found a large dining hall with a long, wooden table and piles of food. He ignored the pies and turkey and roasted carrots, taking a small knife from one of the plates instead. He didn't know exactly how he would use the things he carried with him, but his ability would make them handy somehow, he was sure.

Somewhere on the same floor, he heard a crash and a yell, then more crashing around. Echo must have found his way out of the moat and into one of the other windows. Jack listened to see if he could tell what was happening, and then he heard something very faintly.

"Help us!" a voice called, sounding distant. "Down here! Hurry!"

Jack ran over to the stairs. He heard it again.

"Help us! Down here! Hurry!" It was coming from below him, somewhere deep within the castle.

Jack started to follow the voice, then stopped himself. "Who's there? Where are you?" he called.

There was no answer for a long time, and then the voice came again, "Help us! Down here! Hurry!"

"What's your name?" Jack called back. "Where can I find you?"

Again, there was no answer for several moments. Then, again, "Help us! Down here! Hurry!"

Jack considered this for a moment, and then ran back upstairs, leaving the voice behind. On the next floor, he found Echo, who appeared to have just finished fighting... something. Whatever it had been was a pile of rubble on the floor now. Echo was breathing hard and covered in mud.

"Where are you going?" Echo asked.

"The prisoners are in the basement, I heard them yelling," Jack said. "But I need help to free them."

Echo didn't say anything, and he didn't rush over. He looked at Jack suspiciously. Jack looked back at him with equal suspicion, but a little bit of a smile, too.

"How did you know?" Echo asked.

"You're better at talking than listening," Jack said. "Your fake prisoners didn't answer any of my questions. Neat you can send your voice that far, though."

Jack ran up the stairs and Echo chased after him. Jack had a head start, but Echo was faster. By the time they reached the top of the largest tower, they were right next to each other and both out of breath.

They were met by a thick, wooden door with a stone handle. When Jack tried to open it, it refused to budge. Without warning, Echo let out a shriek that blasted the door to splinters. Jack barely got out of the way.

"Hey, watch out!" Jack protested.

"I'm fine," Echo countered. "*You* watch out."

Echo ran into the prison cell first, and Jack followed him.

"What the heck is this?" Echo asked.

In the center of the room sat two small stone statues, each with chains around the wrists. Each of them wore a bright tunic: one with the symbol of The Empty Hand and the other with the symbol of The Steel Heart.

Jack studied the statues carefully. He needed a way to break the chains without damaging the statue. He took out the scepter he had found earlier, delicately using it as a makeshift hammer. The chains snapped easily with the first blow.

"You take your time, I'm out of here!" Echo said. He yelled toward the chains on his statue, intending to break them. It worked. Both chains shattered—and so did the statue.

"That's not fair!" Echo yelled, rattling the castle. "Now what do I do?"

Jack knew it was time to run. He grabbed his statue and hurried to the stairs.

Echo tried to scoop up the remains of his stone prisoner, but it was hopeless. "Well if I can't win, I'll make sure you can't either!"

Echo ran after Jack and quickly gained ground. He yelled down the stairs, blasting pieces out of them. Jack jumped to the railing, sliding down it expertly while Echo struggled over the damaged stairs behind him.

On the main floor, the drawbridge was still closed. Jack could hear Echo yelling behind him, blasting away carelessly. Jack knew he wouldn't have time to find the levers that let the bridge down. He took out the knife he'd found in the dining hall and threw it toward the heavy rope holding up the bridge. The knife found its mark and sliced cleanly through the rope.

The drawbridge fell suddenly, hitting the ground on the other side of the moat with a thud so loud Jack was sure it would break... but it held. He ran across the bridge and through the field toward Mr. Hart and the waiting students. Echo chased him, kicking up large sprays of dirt with his screams as he tried to break Jack's statue. But Jack resisted the urge to run straight to Mr. Hart and the other students and instead focused on leaping and rolling out of the way.

He made it! Behind him, Echo let out a final, piercing wail, but Mr. Hart waved a hand, shielding himself and the students. Realizing he had lost, Echo gave up and rejoined the students, refusing to look anyone in the eye.

"Commendable," Mr. Hart said to Jack. "You thought and acted carefully, and defeated an opponent who was faster, stronger, and more experienced. Sometimes a situation calls for acting quickly, but more often, caution and consideration will win the day. It's good to keep your wits about you, even when you need to rush." He looked over at Echo. "Although you're growing into a talented young man, you'd best learn how to control both your attitude and aggression. It is important for one to have confidence and ambition, but there is a fine line between those two and arrogance, which when crossed, will cause you much more harm than gain."

"Yes, sir," Echo said quietly.

"Now, each team has two points. How exciting. One final competition will decide the winner. Meet me back here—at midnight."

Mach and the Void of Space

Mach took a deep breath and checked his outfit. Everything was in place. He would know if it wasn't, but it still made him feel better to physically look over everything. To his classmates he looked a bit strange, as he was covered in a seemingly random assortment of electronics: cell phones, batteries, radios, and three laptops in a bulky backpack. To other people it was junk, but they didn't see machines the way Mach did.

Ever since he was young, he could hear them. Perhaps "hear" wasn't the right word, since they didn't make a sound, but something inside Mach could feel their energy and know whether they were happy or sad, excited, or calm. He could also use his mind to tell them what to do, and they would listen to him. He didn't force them—Mach always thought the machines just liked that someone was paying attention, and so they agreed to work with him. His friend Tink had been very curious about his ability and how it worked, but the truth was Mach didn't know. It just did.

He stood in the moonlight in the courtyard, along with Mr. Hart and the other students. He wasn't sure why the contest was taking place at night, but he'd slept all day to be ready for it. The student next to him, a boy named Titan, was ready as well. He looked like he was ready for anything. Even though they were the same age, Titan was easily twice as large as any other student and absolutely full of muscles. But he moved lightly, often skipping or floating from place to place. On top of his amazing strength, Titan could fly, and he was invulnerable.

To make matters worse, if he lost, his team would lose the whole thing. The machines chittered to him in reassurance, but even though he was confident in his own abilities, he knew Titan could do almost anything.

"You could have requested to participate in the sparring battle and won easily, you know," Mach said to him.

"Maybe," Titan said with a shrug of his giant shoulders. "But there are plenty of things you can do when you're strong besides fight. Better things, honestly."

Titan prided himself on being gentle and careful—he didn't want to intimidate or hurt anyone. He had a bubbly, gentle personality and was always willing to help. It caught his classmates off guard at first, but they quickly realized they shouldn't judge Titan by his looks but rather by his behavior. Mach had asked Titan for help on a few occasions, and it was always gladly given.

"I hope you are enjoying the night," Mr. Hart said, calling them to attention. "I think you'll agree it is quite beautiful."

It was, in fact, a wonderful night to be outside. The air was warm and the sky was clear, sparkling with countless stars. The moon loomed large in the sky, its light giving the courtyard a mysterious but comforting glow. Mach privately wished that, instead of a competition, he could lay on his back stargazing until the sun came up.

"This is the final competition," Mr. Hart said, speaking directly to Mach and Titan. "I have planted a flag, and it is your job to retrieve it. Since the two of you will be leaving the academy grounds, I want to reiterate that I personally approved you to participate in this contest. I believe and expect that you will be careful and safe when you leave. I also believe you are both capable of achieving the task at hand."

"Yes, sir," Titan said. Mach nodded in agreement.

"Tonight, you'll be going to the Moon," Mr. Hart said.

The other students whispered among themselves. Even for them, with all their abilities, it seemed like an impossible task. Although, if anyone could do it, it was Mach and Titan. Titan could breathe in space and Tink had outfitted Mach with a thermal suit that was based on space suits, because they'd hypothesized, he might have to climb a mountain or travel somewhere extreme. But no one had expected something like this.

Mach and Titan looked at each other.

"Let's make a deal," Titan said. "I have good enough vision that I'll be able to see you, if you stay lit up. And if you give me one of your machines, you'll be able to hear where it is, right? That way if either of us need help, we'll be able to find each other."

Mach thought about it. He liked the idea of a safety net, and Titan didn't seem like the type of person to try and trick him.

"Deal," Mach said. A tiny handheld video game beeped in affirmation, and Mach handed it to Titan, who stuffed it in a zippered pocket. "I'd like that back later. But it's good to be safe."

"Of course," Titan said. "I'll see you on the moon. Hopefully I'll be waiting

73

for you."

Mach could feel his suit humming with excitement. It was full of energy and ready to be used. Mach had no idea if he even had enough energy to make it all the way to the moon and back, but the suit didn't seem worried. He'd never gone wrong trusting his machines so far.

Mr. Hart waited for the chatter to quiet down, then spoke up again. "I wish you the best of luck, and I will be watching over you."

"I'll see you there," Titan said. Then, with a whoosh of wind, he leapt into the air, scattering dust behind him.

"Okay, friends, let's see what we can do," Mach told his suit.

The machinery buzzed and crackled with excitement, although only Mach could hear it. The machines talked to each other just as much as they talked to Mach, and after a few moments they sputtered to life. A powerful fusion core embedded in the suit sent power to the rockets in his boots. There was a burst of smoke, and Mach was flying.

He was surprised by how quickly everything disappeared behind him. His friends shrank to the size of cats, then mice, then ants, and finally they were no longer visible at all.

Outer space was quiet, peaceful, and lonely. Without a good frame of reference, it was difficult to tell how much farther he would have to go, but he knew it was a very long way. Mach's machines would keep him warm and pointed in the right direction, but he would need a lot of patience.

At first, Mach was struck by the beauty of space. Now that he wasn't surrounded by light from Earth, the sparkling stars were brighter than ever and more numerous than he had imagined. He could even see beautiful nebulae that he had previously only seen in pictures. The emptiness of space didn't feel that empty at all—it was him, his machines, and the universe, sharing something together in the silence.

Mach was glad he had his things with him. They buzzed and clicked and hissed as they worked, shared information, or simply made noise for the joy of it. On Earth, it was sometimes a struggle to hear them, because there was always wind blowing or leaves rustling or someone talking. Out here the machines were loud and clear, and kept him occupied as the hours passed.

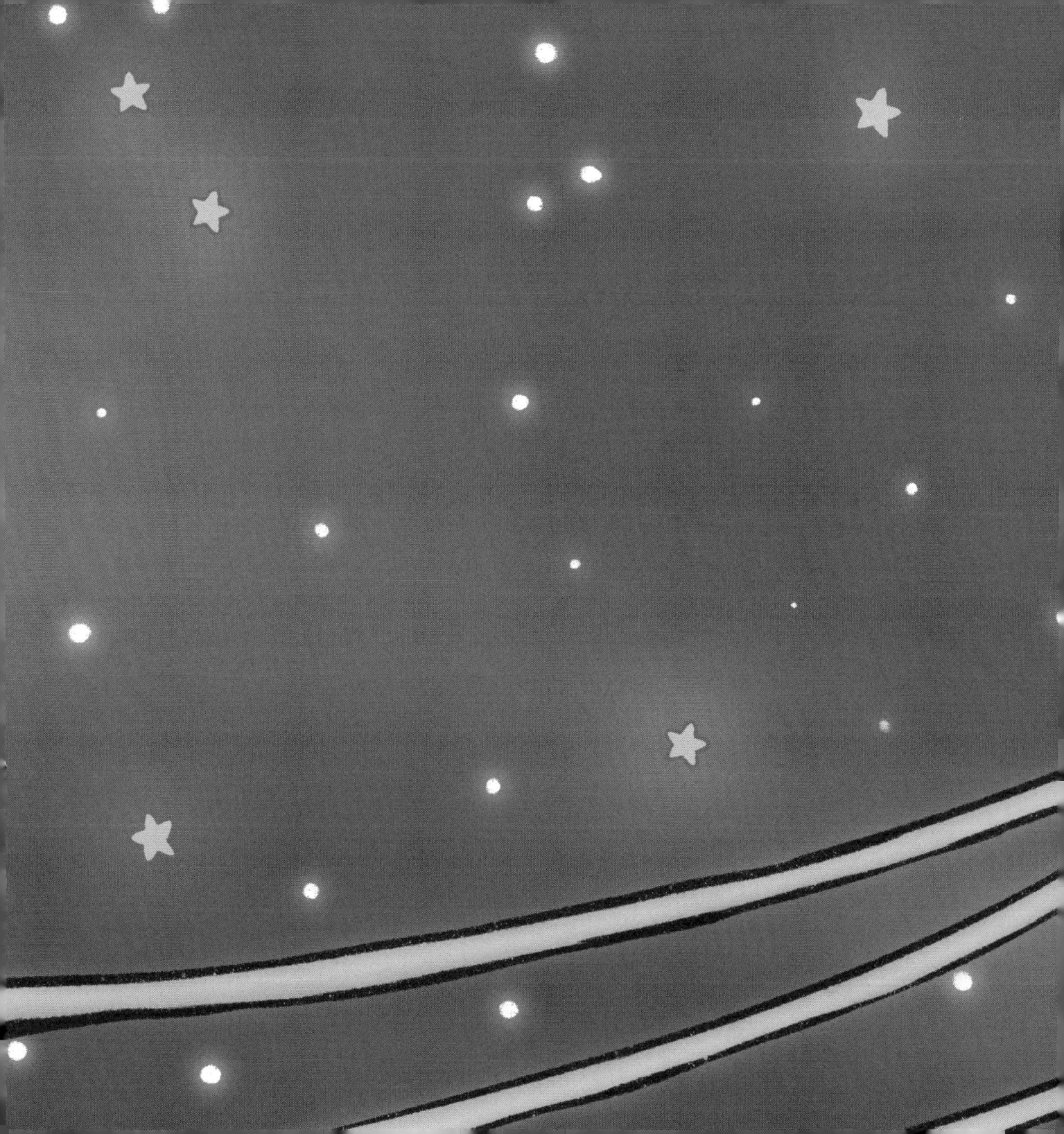

He wondered how Titan was doing. The game Mach had given him called out regularly. It was faint, but it let Mach know that Titan was in front of him somewhere. Mach wasn't worried about being behind for the moment, since the Moon was a long journey away, and he was already going as quickly as he could without overworking his equipment anyway.

Eventually, boredom crept in. Maybe it had been a few more hours, or maybe it had been a dozen. He considered consulting his equipment but decided against it. If he looked now, it would be tempting to look again, and again, and again, until he was checking every minute on a journey that could take days. Mach realized then that not only did he have to go all the way to the Moon, but he'd also have to come all the way back home, thinking about his victory—or his defeat—the whole time.

Mach checked to make sure his equipment would keep him moving toward the Moon, got confirmation, and then closed his eyes. It was hard to relax with the excitement and nervousness of being *in outer space*. But he took deep, even breaths until he fell asleep.

He woke with a jolt. He had a moment of panic until he remembered where he was. He wasn't sure how long he had been asleep, but his electronics reported that there was nothing wrong. They noted Mach's increased heart rate and breathing and helped him calm down. There was more good news as well: He was still behind Titan, but he was closer than before.

"Maybe he's stopping when he needs to sleep," Mach said to himself. "Or maybe he's just getting tired." Mach didn't even know if Titan could get tired. He knew what Titan was capable of, but he wasn't familiar with how Titan's powers actually worked. Instead of worrying about it, Mach simply enjoyed his good fortune and stayed on his path.

The next day—if that was even the right word—was much the same. He admired the beauty around him, stayed patient, listened to his equipment, checked on Titan, and eventually became bored again. He tried to play games in his mind: doubling numbers, rhyming words together, or imagining intricate stories. Eventually, he couldn't think of anything else at all, so he slept again.

When he woke the next time, the moon looked much larger than he remembered it before. It was still hard to tell how far he had to go or how long it would take, but he had the feeling he was close. On top of that, Titan was behind him now. Even though they were going to the same place, there was so much space and darkness around them that Titan might not even know he'd been overtaken.

Then, he noticed it: a distress signal. It was coming from the game he'd given Titan. It wasn't life or death, and Titan wasn't hurt, but he needed help. Mach wasn't sure what to do, and from the sounds coming from all his equipment, his machinery wasn't sure what to do either. Some of them wanted to continue on to win, and help Titan on the way back, while others thought they should go to Titan right away. Mach didn't think Titan was too far away, but if he was backtracking now, his chances of winning might disappear.

He looked back toward Earth, then to the Moon, then back to Earth again. He was hoping he would see something that would help him make the decision—maybe Titan floating behind him, or the flag on the moon in front of him. He didn't see anything that would point him one way or the other. All he had were the rules for the contest and the steady, chirping distress signal coming from Titan's direction.

Maybe he was naive. Maybe it was a trick or a mistake. But if he was part of the Hidden Grove Academy to learn to be a hero, it felt wrong to leave someone floating alone in space. Even someone as strong as Titan, and even if it were to cost his team the victory. Mach turned away from the moon and toward his friend.

At first, Mach didn't see anything. But he kept following the distress signal, and it kept getting louder. Eventually, he could see Titan in the distance. Titan was moving toward the moon, but slowly. Mach couldn't imagine how long it would take his friend to get to the Moon at that pace. When Titan saw Mach approaching, relief flooded his face. He tried to say something, but without any air, there wasn't any sound. Titan pointed to the Moon, then back to Earth, and shrugged.

Mach uncoiled a thick cord and handed one end to Titan. Titan smiled weakly and gave him a thumbs-up. They moved toward the Moon together, with Mach towing Titan behind him. Within a few hours, they touched down.

Titan laid down immediately, impervious to the cold. He closed his eyes but stayed awake, enjoying the rest. Mach wasn't sure what to do. The minutes passed and he considered going to look for the flag, but he didn't want to leave his friend alone. After a few more minutes, Titan sat up and used his finger to trace a message in the dusty lunar surface. *So tired,* it read. Then Titan added, *Never been tired before.*

Mach was surprised. On Earth, it always felt like Titan had power without limit. But, Mach supposed, Titan had never exerted himself so much before. *You okay?* Mach wrote back. Titan nodded.

They sat quietly, looking at the stars, the surface of the Moon, or the Earth, a vibrant blue-green world suspended in the void of space. *Beautiful,* Titan wrote. Mach nodded. Titan added to his message. *I like the quiet.*

Mach pointed to the various gadgets that adorned him and shrugged. He'd been surrounded by beeps and buzzes and clicks as long as he could remember.

All the time? Titan wrote. Mach nodded. *Wow,* Titan wrote.

Mach had an idea. It made him nervous, but he decided to do it anyway. He shut down as many machines as he could. He had to leave a few on to keep oxygen flowing, water recycling, and warmth circulating, but everything nonessential got turned off. It was uncomfortable at first. He wanted to hear the noises again, familiar and safe. However, he remembered Mr. Hart had told him that without change, one cannot grow as an individual, even though change was always uncomfortable at first.

Titan put one hand on Mach's shoulder and used his other to make a wide, sweeping gesture to the stars. They both laid down and looked up. Very few people got to see the world—the universe—the way Mach and Titan were getting to see it. The contest seemed like a small distraction now. This was worth so much more.

They rested for a long time, and then Titan sat up and stretched. *Home?* he wrote.

Flag? Mach wrote back.

Titan shrugged, then nodded. They got up together. Mach enjoyed hopping along on the surface of the moon, sailing upward with ease and then floating back down. He wondered if this was how Titan felt on Earth.

The first time Titan hopped, he jumped so high he tumbled upward into space. Mach was worried and was ready to go after him. But Titan flew back down to him, laughing soundlessly. He soon got used to the lower level of gravity. The two of them explored together. It was probably faster to fly up and look around, but they had fun playing together on the surface instead.

Titan spotted the flag first and pointed toward it. Mach looked in the direction Titan showed him, then back at Titan, raising his eyebrows. Titan gave him a friendly shrug, and without exchanging any words, they decided they would go to the flag together.

The flag didn't have the symbol of The Empty Hand or The Steel Heart. Instead, it had the symbol of the academy: a large tree with a wide, sheltering canopy. Titan plucked the flag from the dirt and the two boys shared a celebratory fist bump. Mach turned all his equipment back on and they flew home together, with Mach towing Titan whenever he got tired.

When they landed back at Hidden Grove, Mach pulled off his helmet and took a giant breath of fresh air. His legs felt heavy and rubbery, and he sat down immediately.

"It's good to be back," he said. "But I'm starving."

Titan stuck the flag into the dirt. It was so early that it was still dark. Titan flew off in a flash, then returned with a pile of fruit—apples, oranges, bananas, whatever he'd found in the school's kitchens. They ate hungrily.

The sky lightened gradually as the sun rose. In its own way, it was as beautiful as gazing out into the whole universe. Mach was glad he was taking the time to enjoy it.

A student came outside and noticed them, and Mach recognized Echo, one of Titan's teammates. Echo turned toward the school and yelled, "They're here! They're back from the Moon! Everyone, wake up!" His voice carried to every corner of the school, waking all their classmates and Mr. Hart as well.

Students in pajamas tumbled outside, sleepy but eager to hear stories of their journey. Everyone wanted to know what it was like, what had happened, and who had won. The boys described everything, including the fact that neither of them had won.

After more stories and some lighthearted arguments over the winner, Mr. Hart arrived. He was put together, wearing a dark suit with a green tie. While always quite personable, he was not the type to arrive in pajamas.

"I am extremely proud of the two of you," Mr. Hart said. He didn't ask them for any details and seemed to simply know what had happened, but no one questioned it. They were used to that sort of thing from Mr. Hart. "Your contest has ended in a draw, so I will award a point to each of you."

A few of the students protested and started to argue. Some said that Mach should be declared the winner, because he was in the lead and had to help Titan make it to the Moon. Others pointed out that Titan should be the winner because he had physically touched the flag first.

Mr. Hart raised a hand and waited for them to be quiet. "Yes, this means the final score is three for each team. Everyone performed exceedingly well, whether or not they won their individual event. You should be impressed with yourselves, not disappointed."

He waited a moment to see if anyone would protest, but no one did. "I'm happy to see you all so invested in the games, but it is very early," Mr. Hart continued. "Get some sleep, have some food, and we'll have the closing ceremony this afternoon at one o'clock. I'm sure you're all very excited right now, but it's important to get some rest."

At first the students hung around, eager to talk to Mach, Titan, and to each other. But Mr. Hart looked at them pointedly until each of them decided to return to bed and only Mach, Titan, and Mr. Hart remained.

"I was worried this one might be too much of a challenge," Mr. Hart said.

"But I believed in you, and it appears that my belief was justified. You were able to undertake a long and difficult task, even when the excitement of it wore off. I'm glad you took the time for contemplation. People would be better off, I think, if more of them were mindful like that."

The boys nodded quietly in agreement. It was hard to express in words how it had felt, to really spend time with their own thoughts.

"It truly is beautiful out there," Mr. Hart added after a long moment of silence. "It always reminds me how special and beautiful our Earth is, too. But, you two need more rest than anyone else, so don't stay up too long." He started to walk away and then turned back to them. "Oh, and when you decide you want to visit the Moon again, make sure you let a teacher know first, so we can help you if you need it."

"Yes, sir," the boys said together, already looking forward to more calm and quiet moments in the future.

Mr. Hart and the Final Test

It was time for the closing ceremony and the students had made their way to the edge of the school grounds. Many of the students were standing together in pairs, although still in close proximity to everyone else. Tink and Aura weren't standing next to each other, but they shared their thoughts back and forth and laughed at jokes only they could hear. Everyone, no matter where they decided to wait, was wondering how things would proceed.

No one expected the competition to end in a tie. They didn't even know it was possible. With five contests, it seemed certain one side or the other would end up with the most points. But after days of anxious waiting, the race to the Moon and back had ended in a draw. Mr. Hart accepted this result and told the students they should get some rest.

Scale suspected that Mr. Hart already knew what had happened on the Moon, but perhaps making the students wait to hear the story from their teammates was a lesson in its own right. Everyone responded differently. Some of them tried to carry on with their day as though they weren't concerned, while others barely slept or ate, filled with nervous energy. Still others busied themselves with schoolwork or other distractions to try to pass the time. But now it was the final ceremony, where Mr. Hart would announce the victors and they would all celebrate.

Mr. Hart walked out onto a stage that he created with his mind as he walked up the steps. The podium assembled itself before he reached it. It was huge and ornate, made of smooth pink stone. There was an image of a kitsune (a nine-tailed fox with powerful magic) delicately carved into it. Allegedly, she had been the one to build the Hidden Grove Academy over a thousand years ago. For almost as long, students had been arguing over whether the story was real or just a myth.

Mr. Hart did not keep them in suspense. "Each of you, win or lose, have done a truly impressive job. You should all be proud. You've demonstrated bravery, patience, quick thinking, compassion, sportsmanship, and more. But there is a crucial skill that remains untested. Teamwork."

Smoke began to appear around Mr. Hart. It rose into the air, and Mr. Hart began to grow. As he did, his skin became stone and turned black as coal. His eyes began to burn orange-yellow. They looked like small, fiery suns set inside a living mountain.

"Defeat me, and I will declare each of you the winner." Smoke poured from the monster's mouth as Mr. Hart spoke, revealing a powerful furnace within. "Win or lose—you must do it together."

Echo didn't wait for a second. "Let's go!" he cried, running headlong at the giant.

Echo let out a wild yell. Mr. Hart lifted a giant arm to stop the incoming blast and fell back a step. Everyone cheered. Mr. Hart, surprisingly fast for a stone giant, swung his arm at Echo. At the last moment, Fade blinked close, grabbed Echo, and pulled him out of the way.

"Stay on the attack!" Fade said to him. "That's what you're good at, right? I'll keep you safe."

Titan took to the air, flying straight at the giant's head. Mr. Hart breathed a jet of hot flames right at him, but Titan, invulnerable, flew through it and delivered a powerful punch that made Mr. Hart stumble backward and then fall, sending dust and debris flying in all directions.

"I can't see anything!" Mach yelled.

Tink sprung into action, running to one of his supply closets and grabbing one of his powerful fans. Originally, he'd thought to use them in a flying suit, but he had never finished it. He fired up one of the fans, and the dust began to clear.

Jack ran over and grabbed the other fan to help.

"Thanks!" Tink said. "You just—"

Jack fired it up without help. "Got it!" he said with a wide smile.

Splendor and Echo both blasted Mr. Hart, who was attempting to stand back up. He got to his feet just in time to see Titan flying at him again with a punch that would surely end the fight.

Mr. Hart let out a mighty roar, then clapped his powerful hands together. There was a blast of heat and a shockwave that sent them all flying through the air or tumbling to the ground.

Their ears rang so loudly that no one could hear a thing. They were scattered around, looking to see if anyone was still standing.

Okay everyone, Aura thought to her classmates. *If you're hurt, move to the back so*

Grace can heal you. Everyone else, get ready for a frontal attack. Scale, I need you.

Everyone gathered for a final, last-ditch effort.

What can I do? Scale thought to Aura.

You can win this for us, Aura thought back. *Sneak around behind Mr. Hart and climb up his back.*

Then what am I supposed to do? Scale thought with a dismayed look. *He's made of stone!*

Get creative, Aura thought. *If you can distract him for a moment, we can do the rest.*

Scale was not convinced, but he could see everyone else grouping together so he ran to his spot. Mr. Hart didn't notice him at all, since he was paying attention to the group. "Let's go!" Echo yelled. A few students could hear him faintly and started to move.

Wait! Aura thought at them. *Wait for my signal!* She could see them getting antsy, so she kept repeating herself. *Wait. Wait. Wait.* They listened.

Scale leaped onto the giant's back and climbed toward his head. Mr. Hart roared and turned toward Scale, then tried to shake him off, but Scale held on.

Now! Aura thought. She didn't have to repeat herself. They ran and flew at Mr. Hart, blasting him with energy beams and sound waves and punches and everything else they could muster. Scale held on tight until the last moment, diving away with a roll just before the attacks took their headmaster to the ground. With a final loud yell, Mr. Hart collapsed to the ground in a huge cloud of smoke.

When they could see again, Mr. Hart was on the ground and back in his human shape. And he was laughing.

"Truly spectacular!" he said, congratulating them. "I haven't fought anyone that strong in a very, very long time. All of you have won because you worked together. I saw each of you doing your part individually, but it's how you relied on each other that was special. You're far greater together than you are apart. I didn't stand a chance."

Mr. Hart let the students revel in their victory. He knew that their bravery, quick thinking, compassion, and cooperation would someday form them into an unstoppable superhero team. But, he thought, it was okay to let them finish school first.

Leave Your Feedback on Amazon

Please think about leaving some feedback via a review on Amazon. It may only take a moment, but it really does mean the world for small businesses like mine.

Even if you did not enjoy this title, please let us know the reason(s) in your review so that we may improve this title and serve you better.

From the Publisher

Hayden Fox's mission is to create premium content for children that will help them expand their vocabulary, grow their imaginations, gain confidence, and share tons of laughs along the way.

Without you, however, this would not be possible, so we sincerely thank you for your purchase and for supporting our company mission.

Made in United States
Troutdale, OR
06/08/2023